The Stages of Change Workbook

Practical Exercises For Personal Awareness and Change

James E. Phelan, MSW, Psy.D

To order additional copies visit:
www.createspace.com/4575536

Copyright © 2014
James E. Phelan
Practical Application Publications
Printed in the USA. Charleston, SC
All rights reserved.
ClipArt, Copyright © 2004 Microsoft Corporation

No portion of this publication may be reproduced in any manner
without written permission of the author or publisher.

ISBN-10: 0-9779773-3-1
ISBN-13: 978-0-9779773-3-8

Dedicated to all the men and women I have had the privilege to help in their change processes over the past 20 years.

About the Author

James E. Phelan received his doctorate degree in psychology from the *Southern California University for Professional Studies* and his master's degree from *Marywood University*. He is a Board Certified Diplomate in Clinical Social Work (BCD) and an Internationally Certified Alcohol and Drug Abuse Counselor (ICADC).

The stages of change workbook:
Practical exercises for personal awareness and change

Table of Contents

	Page
Introduction	v.
Chapter 1: **An outline of the *stages of change***	1
Chapter 2: ***Pre-contemplation***	5

Exercises

How do you describe yourself?	6
Building trust	7
Making and listening to affirmation tapes	8
Nurturing yourself	9
Check out your response system	10
I'd know if I had a problem	12
Warning signs	13
What do I need to change?	14
Readiness for change survey	15
What can I do to be a success?	16
Getting feedback	17
Wellness Inventory	18

Chapter 3: ***Contemplation***	19

Exercises

Ambivalence	20
Talking about change	21
Setting the stage: Daily plan for change	22
Dialoguing with your addiction	23
Map for the future	24
Getting your needs met	25
Assessing the now and then	26
Feeling two ways	27
Help, I am feeling "stuck"!	28
Cost-Benefit analysis	29

Chapter 4: ***Preparation***	30

Exercises

Preparing for change	31
Promises for activation	32
Pick their brain	33
What my behavior needing change took and takes from me	34
Picture this	35
Control	36

Chapter 4: *Preparation* (cont.)   Page

Know thyself	37
Keep a diary/journal	38
What causes me emotional pain?	39
Keeping a mood log	40
Getting real	41
Surrendering to reality	42
Using the I2E2 Model for Lasting Change	43

Chapter 5: *Action*   **44**

Exercises

Action steps	45
Finding a sponsor/mentor	46
Bibliotherapy	47
Moving from unrealistic expectations to realistic expectations	48
Let the feelings flow	49
Forgiving Others	50
Tagging procrastination	51
Understanding group dynamics	52
Rules for getting the most out of group	53
Talking to the group	54
Opening up in a recovery group	55
Relapse prevention plan	56
Recovery plan outline	59
Recovery plan worksheet	64
A deeper look	67
Setting Goals: Using the SMART Model	68

Chapter 6: *Maintenance*   **69**

Exercises

Practicing H.A.L.T	70
Relapse warning signs	71
Stress management	73
Centering	74
What does a healthy support system look like?	75
Journaling	76
Identifying my support network	77
Asking for forgiveness	78
Good-bye letter to your addiction	79
Become a champion for change	80
Continued growth and development	81

Chapter 7: *Relapse/relapse prevention*   **82**

Exercises

Is this what I really want?	83

Chapter 7: ***Relapse/relapse prevention*** (cont.) <u>Page</u>

Preventing future relapse	84
Building coping skills against relapse	85
Identifying high risk situations	86
Identifying problem areas	87
What did relapse teach me?	88
Rebounding from relapse	89
RELAPSE Prevention	90
Reset the clock	91
Warning signs	92
Dress rehearsal	93
References/Suggested readings	**94**
Important contacts	**97**
Journal pages	**98**

Strange fascination, fascinating me
Changes are taking the pace....

Changes
Turn and face the stranger

- David Bowie

Introduction

Congratulations for taking this courageous step forward in your consideration to change, no matter what that change is! The exercises you are about to complete are geared towards stages of change, highly influenced by the Transtheoretical Model of Change and Motivational Interviewing (MI).

Change is a process that unfolds over time through a sequence of fluid stages. Each stage offers unique challenges and opportunities. Without planned interventions however, you will get stuck in early stages; that's why working fully through each stage is vital.

This workbook can be used for your personal journal through whatever stage you may be in. It is best used to accompany counseling, group work, or sponsorship. It's recommended that you process these exercises with someone safe. That "someone" should be a counselor, sponsor, mentor, or clergy who is trained in and familiar with how people change.

These exercises present an inherent challenge to your change process, but be cautious to not get overwhelmed by them. You will find it easier to use a separate notebook to process your work as space is limited within the confines of the book. Some exercises may only take a short while to complete while others may take several days and even months to complete. The important thing is that you have a practical exercise that will meet you where you're at, when you need it.

I wish you the greatest success in your healing journey!

Chapter 1: An outline of the stages of change

According to Prochaska and DiClemente (1984), people pass through a series of stages when change occurs (see Figure 1, pg. 4). Miller & Rollnick (2013) focus on the particular conversations about change that takes place in the various stages of a person's readiness to change. This workbook helps those in any stage to broaden their awareness about change in efforts to facilitate it through practical exercises. The stages of change theory are outlined as follows:

PRECONTEMPLATION (Not ready to change)

- Not currently considering change, but maybe someone else suggested it.
- Not intending to take action in the near future.

    Practical tasks:

    -Assess lack of readiness

    -Evaluate current behavior and ambivalence

    -Self-exploration

    -Personalize risk

CONTEMPLATION (Thinking of changing)

- Ambivalent about change
- Not considering change right away.

    Practical tasks:

    -Evaluate pros and cons of behavior change.

    -Identify and promote new, positive outcome expectations.

PREPARATION (Ready to change)

- Some experience with change and trying to change
- Planning to act soon

    Practical tasks:

    - Take small initial steps

    - Take inventory

- Get involved

ACTION (Making change)

- The active work toward desired behavioral change including modification of environment, experiences, or behavior has been taken.

- At this stage most people have made specific overt modifications in their lifestyles.

- At this stage measures should be taken against relapse.

    Practical tasks:

    - Restructure cues and social support.

    - Enhance self-efficacy for dealing with obstacles.

    - Guard against feelings of loss and frustration

MAINTENANCE (Staying on track)

- The focus is on ongoing, active work to maintain changes made and relapse prevention.

- At this stage people are less tempted to relapse and increasingly more confidant that they can continue their change.

    Practical tasks:

    -Plan for follow-up support

    -Reinforcement of internal rewards

    -Discuss relapse prevention

RELAPSE

- Regression to previous stages.

- Falling back to the old behaviors after going through other stages.

    Practical Tasks:

    -Evaluate triggers for relapse

    -Reassess motivation and barriers

    -Plan stronger coping strategies

    -Reassess and rewrite relapse prevention plan

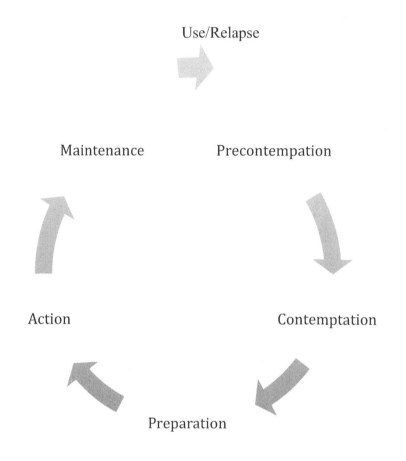

Figure 1: The Stages of Change Flow

Chapter 2   Exercises for pre-contemplation

Practical tasks:

- Assess lack of readiness

- Evaluate current behavior and ambivalence

- Self-exploration

- Personalize risk

How do you describe yourself?

Have you really thought about how you describe yourself? Getting in touch with how you really see yourself can be helpful. If you had to think of 10 words to describe yourself, what would they be?

Use the spaces below or use your notebook to write ten words that you feel describe yourself. Be honest.

1. _____
2. _____
3. _____
4. _____
5. _____
6. _____
7. _____
8. _____
9. _____
10. _____

Which ones do you consider negative? Why?

Which ones are positive? Why?

Is this what you feel others would say about you?

If not, what would be the difference?

What would you like to change and what could be an action plan?

Building trust

Many people do not trust. This often stems from childhood experiences. It can be used as a way of protection and as a way to continue dysfunction. Part of trusting others is to let go of the past. In this exercise you can process what trust means to you and how you can obtain it in your life.

1. What does trust mean to you?

2. What is the connection, or lack of connection, of trusting others and you?

3. Write an inventory of all the experiences you had trusting others.

4. Ask those of whom you are going through life with, "Why should I trust you?"

5. What are your reservations about trust? What holds you back from being fully trustful of others?

6. What are some ways to increase your trust? Can you start asking for what you need?

Making and listening to affirmation tapes

Affirmations are important in personal growth and discovery. Try this exercise: 1) Write a letter about how you would have liked to have been treated as a child growing up by your father, mother, siblings, and peers (or others that were involved in your life such as cousins or uncles). 2) Tape-record this in your own words, or have a friend read it on the tape. Play soothing music in the background. 3) Listen to the tape in a relaxed environment. I suggest starting the process by listening to Brenda Schaeffer's CD *Inner reflections: Meditations for the body and heart*, and finally, 4) Process this with someone you trust.

THE STAGES OF CHANGE WORKBOOK

Nurturing yourself

Nurturing yourself has tremendous benefits. It helps to alleviate the stress that you face daily. Here are five steps toward nurturing yourself that you can practice:

1. *Discover what feels nurturing to you* – try journaling to remember times in which you felt particularly nurtured. Gently ask yourself, "What feels nurturing?" After you discover what is nurturing for you, take the time to invest in it.

2. *Resolve any conflicts around nurturing yourself* – discuss your goal of nurturing yourself with the people around you so that they support you in your efforts to nurture yourself.

3. *Give yourself permission to do what feels nurturing* – create the time, space, and energy to nurture yourself by simply giving yourself the permission to do it.

4. *Evaluate if something was nurturing or not* – spend some time evaluating whether your efforts are working.

5. *Be patient with yourself and other people* – like anything new, learning to nurture yourself takes time and effort. Be patient with yourself, and your family, as you learn to nurture yourself.

(Reference: Editor, (2004, March, 16). *The Open Grove Newsletter, 3* (I-12), 2).

6. *Practice an affirmation*:

> For as long as I can remember, I have lived my life for others. Pleasing others was of utmost importance in my struggle to protect my emotional and physical well-being.
>
> As an adult child, I lived my life for others in an attempt to gain approval and love. I consistently put others' needs ahead of my own.
>
> Now I know that living my life solely to please others is emotional starvation….my enslavement demanded I give up more and more of me and take less in return.
>
> Today…I will consider my own needs, desires, and preferences first. Today I will take care of me.

Adapted from Lerner, R. (1990). *Affirmations for the inner child.* Deerfield, FL: Health Communication.

THE STAGES OF CHANGE WORKBOOK

Check out your response system

How do you respond to stimuli? Believe it or not, your response is not a monolithic approach, but rather it is a full systems approach. The system encompasses your physical, emotional, and behavioral symptoms. In this exercise use the list below and grade the symptoms (refer to the Stress Response Index below) that you get when you are stressed out and tested to the limit. Once you identify your symptoms, develop a plan to address them.

STRESS RESPONSE INDEX
0 = This symptom rarely or never occurs.
1 = This symptom occurs occasionally.
2 = This symptom occurs quite often.
3 = This symptom occurs all the time or nearly all the time.

Physiological Symptoms
____ racing or pounding heart
____ rapid breathing with short, shallow breaths
____ cold sweaty palms
____ excessive perspiration
____ asthma attack
____ butterflies in stomach
____ nausea
____ constipation
____ diarrhea
____ dry mouth
____ high blood pressure
____ sudden and urgent need to urinate
____ tics or twitching muscles
____ heartburn/indigestion
____ stomach cramps or pains
____ tremors or shakiness
____ headaches
____ back pain
____ change in appetite
____ impaired sexual function
____ chronic fatigue, exhaustion
____ frequent urination
____ arthritis pain
____ weight change
____ itching
____ dry skin
____ allergy flare-up
____ colds or the flu
____ skin rash
____ other; specify _____

Emotional Symptoms
____ difficulty concentrating
____ feelings of being sad, blue, or down in the dumps
____ feelings of anxiety, panic, or being out of control
____ forgetfulness
____ suspiciousness
____ racing thoughts

Exercise, continued

___ recurring thoughts you cannot get rid of
___ inability to enjoy the things you used to enjoy
___ feeling as if you will explode
___ restlessness
___ diminished ability to daydream or fantasize
___ mood swings
___ decreased interest in sex
___ decreased interest in previously enjoyed foods
___ being withdrawn, socially isolated
___ apathy
___ cynicism
___ other; specify _____

Behaviors
___ erratic work habits
___ increased use of sick time
___ excessive worrying
___ excessive use of alcohol or other drugs
___ excessive accidents or injuries
___ overeating
___ excessive complaints
___ increased craving for tobacco or sweets
___ change in sleep patterns (difficulty falling asleep/waking up more frequently during the night)
___ angry outbursts
___ nightmares
___ lack of punctuality for work and/or other important functions
___ gritting teeth
___ nail biting
___ finger or foot tapping
___ other; specify _____

Action Plan

1. _____
2. _____
3. _____
4. _____
5. _____
6. _____
7. _____
8. _____
9. _____
10. _____
11. _____
12. _____
13. _____
14. _____
15. _____

I'd know if I had a problem

I: In this exercise challenge yourself to complete these sentences within the following spheres:

Relational

At home, with family:
"I'd know if I had a problem if_____

At work:
"I'd know if I had a problem if_____

With friends:
"I'd know if I had a problem if_____

With (fill in_____):
"I'd know if I had a problem if_____

Psychosocial

Financial:
"I'd know if I had a problem if_____

Emotional:
"I'd know if I had a problem if_____

Legal:
"I'd know if I had a problem if_____

Housing:
"I'd know if I had a problem if_____

II: Process your results:

III: What did you learn?:

IV: Develop an action plan:

Warning signs

It's important to track what our warning signs to problems are. In this exercise think about what warning signs you need to be aware of so you can increase awareness and be prepared.

Warning Signs Assessment

I: Answer these questions:

Physical health (what symptoms do I need to be concerned about?):

Mental/emotional (am I experiencing any changes in my mood?):

Future-oriented (how does the future look to me?):

Activity (am I keeping activity as I should; has my activity motivation decreased?):

Appetite (am I eating right?):

II: Based on your answers above, are you seeing any warning signs that concern you? Any you need to change?

What do I need to change?

What we see and think of ourselves, and our actions, is really subjective. What others see and think is objective. It can be a value to compare the two.

I: For this exercise, ask 2 or more mature and trustworthy people to assess you. Obviously, these people must know you fairly well. Here are the key questions you want to ask yourself and those you have chosen:

Ask yourself: What do I see that I need to improve on, or change?

Ask others: What do you see that I need to improve on, or change?

II: What are the comparisons?

III: Based on these responses, process what you have learned and then develop an action plan based on the changes you want to make.

THE STAGES OF CHANGE WORKBOOK

Readiness for change survey

In this exercise, complete the *University of Rhode Island Change Assessment Scale* (URICA). The survey is free in the public domain under:

http://www.ncbi.nlm.nih.gov/books/NBK64976/#A62297

or,

http://www.uri.edu/research/cprc/Measures/urica.htm

Each statement describes how you feel approaching problems in you life. Indicate the extent to which you tend to agree, or disagree with each statement. In each case, make your choice in terms of how you feel right now, not what you have felt in the past or would like to feel. There are FIVE possible responses to each of the items in the questionnaire:

1 = Strongly Disagree
2 = Disagree
3 = Undecided
4 = Agree 5 = Strongly Agree

Example:

Question/statement   Response

1. As far as I'm concerned, I don't have any problems that need changing. _____

What can I do to be a success

Felgen (2007) stated wisely, "If we pay attention to our problems we'll get more problems; if we pay attention to our successes we'll get more success" (p. 25). In this exercise think about what it takes for you to be successful.

1. What would "success" look like for me?

_____
_____
_____
_____
_____

2. What will I do to be successful: What is my plan of action?

_____
_____
_____
_____
_____

3. How will I know I am a success?

_____
_____
_____
_____
_____

Getting Feedback

Sometimes we can learn about ourselves from others. We can get their insights and formulate truths about ourselves helping us to improve our well-being. Assign the questions below to those closest to you:

Please list my strengths:

_____
_____
_____
_____
_____
_____
_____

Please list those things you see in me that need improvement:

_____
_____
_____
_____
_____
_____
_____

What suggestions do you have for which I can build my strengths:

_____
_____
_____
_____
_____
_____
_____

What suggestions do you have for which I can improve any weaknesses:

_____
_____
_____
_____
_____
_____
_____

Wellness Inventory

Part 1: Take some time to complete the following inventory designed to assess what wellness items are of a desire for you:

Wellness Item:	Desired change: Yes/No	Desired Start Date:
Limit Stress		
Cut down/quit tobacco use		
Eat better		
Manage my weight		
Increase physical activity		
Be more active in my health care		

Part 2: Based on your responses, complete a goal plan:

Be as specific as possible: what, how much, where, how often.

Example: If you indicted you wanted to increase physical activity, a specific goal could be:

"I will exercise at the gym 3 times a week for 20 minutes each time in the morning before work".

(See also exercise: "Setting Goals: Using the SMART Model" pg. 68)

Chapter 3   Exercises for contemplation

Practical tasks:

-Evaluate pros and cons of behavior change.

-Identify and promote new, positive outcome expectations.

Ambivalence

Ambivalence is normal when thinking about change. For example, on one hand you sense some need for change. Perhaps a friend or family member is nagging you, or legal consequences have occurred. On the other hand however, the behavior brings some pleasure, satisfaction, relief, or simply some familiarity. The latter is what Miller and Rollnick (2013) refers to as the *status quo*. This is the part of you that doesn't want to change, because changing the *status quo* is usually hard and uncomfortable. In this exercise you will assess ambivalence by listing what are the pro and cons for changing, and for not changing. Compare the two and use this as a discussion with yourself, counselor, coach, or mentor who can listen respectfully.

Change

Pros: _____
_____
_____
_____
_____
_____
_____

Cons: _____
_____
_____
_____
_____
_____
_____

No change

Pros: _____
_____
_____
_____
_____
_____
_____

Cons: _____
_____
_____
_____
_____
_____
_____

Talking about change

Miller and Rollnick (2013) claim that, "people are more likely to be persuaded by what they hear themselves say" (p. 13). To help facilitate how you might discuss change the authors developed 5 intriguing questions (Miller & Rollnick, 2013, p. 11) and are copied below. For this exercise, honestly answer these questions and record them. Reflect on them yourself, or share with someone else such as a counselor, coach, or mentor who can listen respectfully:

1. "Why would you want to make this change?"

2. "How might you go about it in order to succeed?"

3. "What are the three best reasons for you to do it?"

4. "How important is it for you to make this change, and why?"

5. "So what do you think you'll do?"

THE STAGES OF CHANGE WORKBOOK

Setting the stage: Daily plan for change

Considering change is hard. Each day is a new beginning and should be dedicated to exercise time for your edification. Everyone is different, so the results of this particular exercise will look different for everyone. It is a dual phase approach: 1) Wake up and ask yourself: "What will I do today that considers change?" and 2) "What tools will I need?"

Your tools can be a variety of people, places, and/or things. They are the mechanisms in which you will put your desires into action. Use the outline below to guide you.

1. What will I do today that considers change?

_____
_____
_____
_____
_____
_____

2. What tools do I need?

_____
_____
_____
_____
_____

3. What is my plan of action? What exercise(s) in this workbook can I work on today?

_____
_____
_____
_____
_____
_____
_____

Dialoguing with your problem

Dialoguing with your problem; now that sounds strange! While it does sound strange, it has a powerful effect. It allows you to see the problem from both a subjective and objective view. This exercise will allow you to express how you really feel about the behavior you want to change.

On a separate piece of paper, write a letter to the behavior you want to change. This could include:

- Your feelings about it
- How you see it
- What you want from it
- The consequences of it
- Anything else

✓ Next, be the problem and write a response to the issues you raise about it.

✓ Then, write another letter to it in response to what it told you.

✓ How was the second and third letter different from the first?

✓ What did you learn from this exercise?

Map for the future

No one can really predict the future; however you can plan for the future as best as possible. One way to do so is to have some goals, even if they are not detailed. This exercise will help you start to think about your future and get some clarity on what you would like to see happen in your life:

I: List three possible options you'd like to see before you.

1. _____

2. _____

3. _____

II: Imagine yourself five years from now having taken on one of the options. Now let your imagination go and answer the following questions:

1. Where do you live and how do you feel about it?

_____
_____

2. How do you spend your time and how do you feel about it?

_____
_____

3. Describe your relationship with key people in your life:

_____
_____

Getting your needs met

We have both physical and emotional needs as well as spiritual needs. In this exercise you will process what your needs are, what keeps you from doing what is necessary to get them met, and what you *can* do to get them met.

1. What do you need and deserve?

Physical needs: _____

Emotional needs: _____

Spiritual needs: _____

2. What might keep you from doing that which is necessary to get your needs met?

Physical needs: _____

Emotional needs: _____

Spiritual needs: _____

3. What you can do to get your needs met?

Physical needs: _____

Emotional needs: _____

Spiritual needs: _____

Assessing the now and then

In this exercise you will assess the now and then. Make a list of the things you would like to change. Be specific; list particulars such as experiences, or events. Focus on what you do or experience in the situation. If there is not enough space here, use a notebook or separate pages to log your responses.

1. What will happen if you don't make those changes?

2. When you are finished this process, what will be different?

3. What will be (or has been) the first and smallest sign that change is beginning?

4. When you notice that first change, what can you do to keep the ball rolling?

Feeling two ways

Sometimes people feel two ways about something. For example, someone who abuses mood altering substances may feel good on one hand (e.g. the "high"), but on the other may have thoughts about what they are doing is dangerous or illegal, and feel bad. Resolving feeling two ways about something takes some soul searching and usually one path is taken, for better or worse.

I: Is there something you feel two ways about?

If so, in this exercise complete the following questions to help you process feeling two ways:

1. What are the positive/good sides of your feeling?

2. What are the negative/bad sides of your feeling?

II: Rate yourself on the scale on circle where you are more likely to land in your overall feeling:

    0   1   2   3   4   5   6   7   8   9   10
most negative   *most positive*

If you circle "most positive" this means you are less ambivalent and more drawn to the positive/good feeling of your behavior brings you. The positive outweighs the negative. If in the middle you have true ambivalence. If most negative, the negative outweighs the positive. Most people seek change when the negative outweighs the positive.

Where do you land on the scale?

Help, I'm feeling stuck

So maybe you feel like making a change? But, maybe you feel stuck? No worry! This is completely normal. This exercise is designed to help you work through your "stuckness".

Complete the following inventory:

1. What is it I am feeling stuck about?

2. What will it take, or cost to get "unstuck"?

3. Who (what) needs to help me?

4. What is my plan?

Cost-Benefit Analysis

So you have been thinking about change? Thinking through the pros (benefits) and cons (costs) of both changing and not changing is a way to help you fully consider all the possibilities.

In this exercise fill in the appropriate squares in the chart below:

	Benefits (Pros)	Costs (Cons)
Making a Change		
Not Changing		

Chapter 4 Exercises for preparation

Practical tasks:

- Take small initial steps

- Take inventory

- Get involved

Preparing for change

Miller and Rollick (2013) assert that preparatory change talk is best represented by the acronym DARN: Desire, Ability, Reasons, and Need. In this exercise you will process those areas that identify preparatory change talk.

Desire

List any desires for change you have (e.g. "I want to stop drinking"; "I hope I will stop getting arrested"):

_____
_____
_____
_____
_____
_____

Ability

List any perceived ability for change you may have (e.g. "I can..."; or "I am able to..."):

_____
_____
_____
_____
_____
_____

Reasons

List any reasons you would want to change (e.g. "I would feel much better….."):

_____
_____
_____
_____
_____
_____

Need

List why you need to change (e.g. "I need to change because….."):

_____
_____
_____
_____
_____
_____

Promises for activation

Miller and Rollick (2013) assert that commitment to change is the point from which you move from mere desire to persistent will. It is a promise you make you yourself.

In this exercise you have the opportunity to make a committed promise to change. Fill in the space below:

Promise statement

I promise…..
_____
_____
_____
_____
_____

Activation

According to Miller and Rollnick (2013) a promise is one thing but the next level of action is indicating movement toward the promise. Statements such as "I am willing to….." or I'm prepared to…..":

What would your activation statement be:
_____
_____
_____
_____
_____

Pick their brain

List three or more people you know who have had a problem of any type and have been helped. If you don't know of anyone personally, ask someone for referrals.

Go to at least three of these people and, after explaining your situation, ask them for their advice or assistance. Pay attention to any skills they mention that they have used to ameliorate their problems. Record their responses.

- What was instrumental to their recovery?

- What are their strengths?

- What are their weaknesses?

- How has this exercise influenced your thinking about addiction and how it can be solved?

Don't forget to process this with someone!

What my behavior needing change took and takes from me

Behavior comes with a cost. In this exercise you are challenged to think about the many things it took from you and may still be taking from you. Examples include broken marriages, health, finances, emotional wellness, and so on. In the spaces below or in a notebook, list the losses that it dealt you and perhaps is still dealing you.

1. _____
2. _____
3. _____
4. _____
5. _____
6. _____
7. _____
8. _____
9. _____
10. _____

THE STAGES OF CHANGE WORKBOOK

Picture this

Draw two pictures: One with your problem, and one without. Compare and contrast. Process this with someone, or in a group.

With:

Without:

35

Picture this

Control

What do you have control over and what don't you? In this exercise you will be challenged to think about those things you can control and those you can't.

1. Write five or more things about your problem situation that you can control.

    1. _____
    2. _____
    3. _____
    4. _____
    5. _____

2. How do you control each of these things?

    1. _____
    2. _____
    3. _____
    4. _____

3. Write below five or more things about your problem situation that you cannot control.

    1. _____
    2. _____
    3. _____
    4. _____
    5. _____

4. In what ways have you tried to control these things and what has been your degree of success?

    1. _____
    2. _____
    3. _____
    4. _____

Know thyself

Once you acquire self-insight then you are better poised to change. The best strategy is to pay close attention to what others remark about you. It's like playing an investigator. Look and listen and do not get defensive. All this data is constructive.

Log:

- ✓ Pay close attention to remarks and responses from others about you.
- ✓ Collect the data and make notes.
- ✓ Review this with someone and process it.

Ask yourself:

1. What did I learn?

2. What areas can I change?

Keep a diary/journal

Summarizing your daily activities can be very helpful. This process serves to help you unload what's going on each day and provides you an avenue of review so you can see what patterns and trends you are facing. Obtain something you can write in and which you can keep in a safe place. Process your diary or journal with someone periodically. Be honest in your diary or journal. Don't just log in activities, log in your thoughts and feelings as well.

THE STAGES OF CHANGE WORKBOOK

What causes me emotional pain?

It is important to be able to identify your emotional pain and its sources. It is also good to be able to establish a supportive network in which to share this pain. Finally, expressing the pain is one way of healing it. This exercise will help you to accomplish this.

1. Identify and rank five things, or events in your life that have, and continue to cause you the most emotional pain.

2. Explain to someone, or in a group how you dealt with the pain.

3. Next, ask them for feedback. If they have shared the same or similar pain, ask them how they dealt with it.

4. How can you put this information to use to help you?

5. If you could express your pain, how would you do it?

Keep a mood log

Keeping a mood log will help you to track your feelings. In this exercise you will be able to list your moods throughout the day, along with what time of day they occurred, what your were doing at the time, who was around, whether or not your talked about it, your affect, and what you did (intervention). If you did nothing, then you can plan an intervention for the future. The log also helps you to see any patterns that may be occurring.

Mood	Time	Behavior	People	Discuss	Affect	Intervention	Plan
Ex: Sad	*8 pm*	*I was watching TV*	*Husband*	*I didn't talk about it*	*Some tears; sad look*	*I did nothing*	*Talk to a friend, journal*

Getting real

The work of *getting real* is about paying attention to and communicating about what you notice in yourself. This encompasses your bodily sensations, your feelings, your thoughts, and the things going on around you – your awareness. The work or practical application of getting real is sharing with others how you experience your awareness. When we interact with others, we are bound to get bodily sensations, feelings, or thoughts. Allowing ourselves to be aware of these is the first step to getting real. After such, comes the work. That is, sharing with others what is going on within us. The problem, according to Campbell (2001), is that we often stuff our real data. She says, "Instead of sharing our feelings and thoughts, we try to ensure a predictable outcome" (p. 3). The latter, of course, is unhealthy. In those cases we disconnect from the truth of the situation and the truth of our own feelings. Campbell goes on to say that if we persist on trying to get our relationships to conform to our expectations, instead of letting them be how they actually are, we miss the important opportunities to know others and ourselves more deeply. Getting real is about relating. Examine the outlining 10 skills and practice them:

1. *Experiencing what is.* What is refers to whatever is actually going on in the present moment – in our body, mind, and environment. Campbell stressed that we must practice distinguishing between what we actually experience in our body from what our mind thinks, judges, expects, or predicts.
2. *Being transparent.* This involves the use of self-disclosure, which is the ability to reveal to another person what we have done or what we are sensing, feeling, thinking, or saying to ourselves at the moment.
3. *Noticing your intent.* Be spontaneous and unrehearsed in relating to others to get the real emotional affect. Don't communicate with the intent to control the outcome. Let the outcome evolve out of the relationship.
4. *Welcome feedback.* Be actively curious about how others are affected by you. Ask questions such as, "How are you with what I did?"
5. *Assert what you want and do not want.* Asserting what we want affirms our right to want what we want even if that means we may not get it. We must also be able to refuse to do, receive, or speak about something that is not our genuine response.
6. *Taking back projections.* Often what we see in another person is actually a mirror of something in ourselves that we are uncomfortable with. When someone aggressive puts off a timid person, perhaps he disowns his own aggressiveness. Becoming aware of projections helps us to season our judgments with humility. It should serve to remind us that other's judgments of us are as much about them as they are about us.
7. *Revising an earlier statement.* We have to be flexible to go back and let someone know when our feelings have changed, e.g. as to clear things up.
8. *Holding differences.* This involves allowing us to embrace our own viewpoints while at the same time being open to hearing and considering differing views.
9. *Sharing mixed emotions.* It's okay to be both angry and afraid. We should share both. This skill teaches you to let go of your ideas and should about being consistent so that you can experience whatever shows up in your awareness.
10. *Embracing the silence.* Get in the moment – silence is connection. Don't try to predict an outcome, just allow yourself to feel.

Reference: Campbell, S. (2001). Getting Real. Tiburon, CA: HJ Kramer

Surrendering to reality

Narcotics Anonymous (1982) says that, "recovery begins with surrender" (p. 86). Without addiction or unhealthy behaviors, we have a chance to function as useful human beings if we accept the world and ourselves as it is. Part of the surrender is facing reality, facing the problems and limitation in our lives. In this exercise, you will be guided through some questions to help you process surrender and reality.

1. What is it about reality you dislike?

2. What are the conflicts you face about reality?

3. What areas in your life do you need to surrender?

4. Can you be satisfied with not having all the answers or solutions?

THE STAGES OF CHANGE WORKBOOK

Using the I2E2 Model for Lasting Change

While educating healthcare workers Felgen (2009) presented a framework that offers a realistic and practical way to achieve results that don't stop short at just mere vision. I think this framework can be applied to anything in life.

I: The *Action Plan* is as such, starting first with a vision.

Vision (what are the concrete terms as experienced collectively – yourself and others?):
    Example: "My family wants solidarity, all of us need harmony".

_____
_____
_____

Inspiration (who else shares this vision? How can you inspire others?):
    Example: "My spouse also wants to see more unity and has made a lot of strides recently."

_____
_____
_____

Infrastructure (what changes in your daily life would increase the likelihood that this vision would thrive? What are the implications?)
    Example: "My spouse and I set a time aside each day to talk, or do a special event or project together."

_____
_____
_____

Education (what knowledge and skills do I need to learn to achieve my vision?):
    Example: "My spouse and I will attend a couple's retreat and follow up enhancement classes.

_____
_____
_____

Evidence (how will you measure your vision; actual impact and outcomes?
    Example: By 6 months my spouse and I will have attended the retreat and completed at least 5 months of follow up classes. We will be able to compete an assessment to see what changes have occurred.

_____
_____
_____

II: Now, think of a vision you have. Then, apply the I2E2 model you have learned above.

Chapter 5   Exercises for action

Practical tasks:

- Restructure cues and social support.

- Enhance self-efficacy for dealing with obstacles.

- Guard against feelings of loss and frustration

Action Steps

In the exercises "Preparing for change" (p. 31) and "Promises for change" (p. 32) you were given the opportunity to think about preparing for change. Now, *action steps* is what Miller and Rollnick (2013) assert are the specific action toward change.

What do your action *steps* look like (e.g. "Today I did not act out;" "I've attended a support group this week"…..):

Finding a sponsor/mentor

Probably one of the most important elements of recovery and healing is sponsorship/mentoring. You cannot heal alone. One of the most difficult areas in recovery is finding the right allies. One reason is that the struggler finds it hard to ask for mentoring and another is that good sponsors/mentors are hard to come by. While this combination makes it difficult, it is not impossible. This exercise is most likely a process rather than an event. Finding a mentor takes careful choosing and therefore time. A sponsor/mentor must be strong, genuine, warm, nonjudgmental, kind, yet challenging and has resolved his* own hang-ups. A man in recovery should find another man; and for the woman in recovery, another woman. In this exercise you will follow the bullets listed below. Then process how you are going to make this happen in your own life. Use the worksheet below to stage your sponsorship/mentorship:

➢ List up to five ideal people who can help you find a mentor/sponsor.**

➢ List up to five appropriate actual candidates to be your mentor/sponsor.

➢ List their demographics (names, locations, how long you've known them, whether or not they know about your addiction, marital status, affiliations, etc.).

➢ Write what you will say to your mentor/sponsor in asking them to mentor you.

➢ Role-play this with a safe person.

After you have chosen your mentor/sponsor(s), list the person(s) you both will be accountable to and who can also help you facilitate some processing.

---

* For grammatical consistency "his" "he" or "him" are used and refers to human beings of either gender. I have used these pronouns in this exercise or elsewhere for that purpose only and no insensitivity or exclusion is intended.

** If you have trouble identifying candidates, ask for help in forming ideas from support group leaders, clergy, organizations, or other safe sources.

Bibliotherapy

Bibliotherapy is simply reading, specifically self-help materials. There are a lot of helpful materials available. I have included a bibliography at the end of this book. Please go there and review the listings. Choose a book and obtain it. Read it chapter-by-chapter while taking notes. Write down any highlights, as well as any questions you may have. Share this with someone or in a group so you can process it.

Name of material	Reading dates
_____	_____
_____	_____
_____	_____
_____	_____
_____	_____
_____	_____
_____	_____
_____	_____
_____	_____
_____	_____
_____	_____

Moving from unrealistic expectations to realistic expectations

In our visions we sometimes have unrealistic expectations of others and ourselves. This can be a trap toward self-defeating feelings. In this exercise you will start to look at expectations in a different way. In the worksheet below isolate those expectations that may be unrealistic in one column. Then process the subsequent columns to get to a resulting feeling that puts you in a win-win situation:

Unrealistic expectations

Ex.: *"I will be free from this frustration and defeat..."*

Underlying hope

"To be happy; secure…"

Resulting feelings

"Sadness when I am defeated..."

Realistic expectation

"I will be able to get up again. I may not be totally freed now, but I can have victories each day…"

Resulting feeling

"Satisfaction, relief...."

Let the feelings flow

Feelings should be processed, not ignored or covered up. Confront strong feelings openly. If you don't allow feelings to be expressed, they will only leak out in physical, emotional, or mental symptoms. Use the five steps listed below as a guide to processing your feelings.

1. ***Recognize the feeling.*** When a feeling emerges, don't push it away. Instead, stay with it, taking time to identify it. Close your eyes and experience it. Locate the feeling in your body. Can you attach a color or an image to it? Give the feeling a name: for example, *sadness*.

2. ***Express the feeling.*** Say aloud, to yourself or another person, "I am feeling sad about _____."

3. ***Clarify the feeling.*** Examine the feeling further to see what's behind it. In the case of sadness, you are probably mourning the end of something that began with joy and hope, or you may find you are also angry at someone for leaving or dying, thus destroying your dream of a relationship. You may feel guilty for having left or for being the one left. Clarify what the feeling really is all about and it's many components (e.g. "I'm sad, mad, and afraid; and I feel guilty, too").

4. ***Explain the feeling.*** As you go deeper into the feeling, you might find another reason at the core of it. Sadness about an ended relationship, for example may have concealed anger at someone leaving, anger when recognized, may in turn exposed deeply rooted fears of abandonment or rejections. When you can identify and explain the feeling's source, you can begin to respond with new behavior. At this point, you may even want to rename the feeling. Beneath what you once labeled sorrow, for example, may be a deep fear that can be traced to your childhood: "I felt the same way when I was a child when I watched Dad and Mom fight."

5. ***Accept the feeling.*** Feelings are neither good nor bad; they just are. You are not a "good" or "bad" person because you have these feelings. None of us has constant control over what we feel from minute to minute. When you stop judging feelings "good" or "bad," you can learn to accept them. Having accepted your own, you will find it easier to accept the feelings of others as well.

Forgiving others

Forgiveness is an action process in the recovery process. But, at what point do you forgive someone? When do you forgive and how? You may be struggling and asking, "Is it okay not to forgive?" The important thing to keep in mind is that the act of forgiveness releases any burden on your part; it does not necessarily excuse any wrongdoings. For those who are spiritual, forgiveness is a requirement in the brotherhood. In such terms, forgiveness is that you simply write off any debt you feel is owed to you. It You can tell the person what they owe you (getting it off your mind), but not necessarily expecting them to pay, as in many cases they could not pay back for all the pain they caused anyway. This exercise gives you an opportunity to process thoughts on forgiveness.

What do you feel you deserve that would even the score from someone that hurt you?

What price do you pay for holding this debt?

Have you let the other person know what you think they deserve?

If not, could you?

Can the other person give you what you want?

How can you release the burden of the debt, if the person cannot give you what you want?

Tagging procrastination

One of the barriers to recovery is self-defeating procrastination. Many people joke about procrastination, but really it is a serious issue that can yield huge consequences. Psychologist Dr. William Backus, in his book, *Finding the freedom of self control*, lists some common rationalizations for procrastinating.

Review the list given by Dr. Backus and see if any of these apply to you and your recovery. If so, develop an action plan whereas you challenge the rationalization.

Checklist

___ I'm too busy.
___ I have too many things to do.
___ I don't know what to do first.
___ I don't have time.
___ I can't do it well so I won't do it at all.
___ I don't know how.
___ I'm not in the mood to do anything I find disagreeable.
___ I'm too tired.
___ I'm sick of doing that.
___ It's too trivial to bother with – other things are more important.
___ I should do some other things before I start that.
___ Other:_____

Processing Questions

1. Which one(s) do you identify with?

2. What plans can you make to defeat procrastination?

Action Plan

_____
_____
_____
_____
_____
_____
_____

Understanding group dynamics

If you are in the action stage it would be beneficial to get involved with a group process with others who are going through some of the same things as you. For those seeking to abstain for alcohol, as an example, AA is a good choice. At any rate, group work can be very beneficial for anyone in the action stage of change. One thing to be conscious of is the various group behaviors that can arise from yourself and other members. Review the following list of commonly seen group behaviors and take the risk to confront them, if and when, they arise in the group you attend.

1. **Minimizing -** For example: "I only had three beers."

2. **Making fools of others -** By putting others down, we take the focus off ourselves.

3. **Assuming** – For example, "Nobody cares about me anyway." This gives us an excuse to act out, because, "Nobody cares…"

4. **I'm unique** – "No one can tell me what to do." By putting ourselves in a special category, we rob ourselves of help.

5. **Lying** – Confuses, distorts, and takes the focus of the behavior. Subtypes include:

    Commission – making things up that are not true.
    Omission – Leaving out details or sections.
    Assent – presenting others' ideas to look good with no intentions of
        following through.

6. **Blaming** – Permits the build up of resentments and takes the focus of the problem and puts in on others. For example: "The trouble with you is that you are so critical of me. If you weren't, maybe I wouldn't have this problem."

7. **Making excuses -** For example: "I have sex because I am depressed and it makes me feel good," or "The reason I drink is because my husband is so mean to me."

8. **Aggression** – Scaring others by power surges so that they will either agree with us or leave us alone.

9. **Staying in the safety zone** – Withholding information because of the fear of confrontation, embarrassment, or fear of being vulnerable.

10. **Grandiosity** – For example: "I've spilled more booze then you've drank," or "He's had sex with only three people and thinks he's a sex addict."

Rules for getting the most out of group

It is undeniably difficult to assimilate in a group setting, especially when it means you must be vulnerable. The following is a helpful guideline for getting the most out of your group experience:

1. The group as a whole must make a commitment to adhere to confidentiality. That is, what is said in the group stays in the group. It must be a safe container.

2. Participate as fully as possible. The more you put in, the more you'll take out.

3. Feel free to give feedback. Do not pass judgment, but simply state what you see or hear and then what *you* feel.

4. Take "time". Focus on the issues you need to work on.

5. Use "I" statements. Don't say "You always make me feel…", instead simply say, "I feel…."

6. Keep an open mind. Be willing to discover positive and negative, growing and limiting sides of yourself.

7. Remember that the group is a place for progress, not perfection. See it as a safe place to grow.

8. Use the group to practice new behaviors. Don't be afraid to ask for help to role-play issues or to use psychodrama to help you express behaviors and emotions.

9. Pay attention to your own body language and feelings. Don't shut them out.

10. Leave your mask and false self outside the group. Be real!

11. Avoid postponing the risk-taking involved in letting others know you.

12. You "earned" your seat in the group. Don't apologize for your statements.

Talking to the group

Talking for the first time in a group is scary. The following outline are some helpful starting lines that will help break the ice and help get you talking. It is also an exercise for the others in listening.

Hello, my name is_____
The reason I'm here is_____
Right now, I'm feeling_____

When I'm in a new group, I_____
When I'm in a new situation, I usually_____
I'm happiest when_____
When I'm alone, I usually_____
My biggest worry, right now, is_____

I love_____
I feel healthy pride when_____
I feel sad or blue when_____
My feelings get easily hurt when_____
I feel embarrassed when_____
The last thing in the world I want to do is_____

My favorite book is_____
My favorite movie is_____
The person I miss the most is_____

The thing I like best about myself is_____
Toward you, right now, I feel_____
Right now I am feeling_____

Opening up in group

Talking in a recovery group or even one-on-one can be scary and difficult. In this exercise you will be able to identify what is hard to talk about and practice ways to talk more openly. This is aimed to help you:

1. List 10 things in your life that are difficult to talk about.

2. Put them in order from the least threatening to the most difficult to talk about.

3. Talk with just one person you trust the most about the experience and what you may have learned from the experience.

4. Examine your fears while doing this with the reality of actually doing it. You will find you feel much better after talking!

5. Next, starting with the least threatening issue, talk about it in a group setting. Again, examine your fears while doing this with the reality of actually doing it. You will find you feel much better after talking!

6. Continue each time with addressing another issue on your list. After you have tackled all 10, you will see how much better you feel, less threatened and less fearful.

Relapse prevention plan

While relapse to old behaviors is common, you can prevent them. Prevention planning is vital in the action stage. Preventing relapse requires an awareness of our own denial process and the willingness to do something about it. We need to be vigilant about exposing our denial to others and ourselves.

I. You have the information within yourself that tells you the circumstances that can set you up for relapse. Answer the following questions as honestly as you can.

Who are the people you are most likely to be around when you are doing this behavior?

1.

2.

3.

4.

What feelings place you at greatest risk for relapse?

1.

2.

3.

4,

What situations or events place you at risk?

1.

2.

3.

4.

Exercise, Continued

What will be the consequences for you if you relapse?

1.

2.

3.

4.

II. This plan is used in conjunction with your relapse warning signs. Look at your feelings, thoughts, and behavior, and decide what you will do about it (action plan).

Example:

Warning sign:	Hanging around using environments.
Thought/s:	I miss my friends.
Feeling/s:	I feel bored and lonely.
Behavior:	I stopped at the bar just to say hello. I had a soda.
Action Pan:	a. Call my sponsor and talk to him/her about it.
	b. Go to a meeting and talk about it.
	c. Make plans to go to a movie with a sober friend in treatment.

Now, outline your own specific plan using:

Warning sign:

Thought/s:

Feeling/s:

Behavior:

Action Plan: a.

  b.

  c.

Exercise, Continued

Warning sign:

Thought/s:

Feeling/s:

Behavior:

Action Plan:
    a.
    b.
    c.

Warning sign:

Thought/s:

Feeling/s:

Behavior:

Action Plan:
    a.
    b.
    c.

Warning sign:

Thought/s:

Feeling/s:

Behavior:

Action Plan:
    a.
    b.
    c.

Adapted with modifications, from: Olsen, J., Fallon, J., & Mark, L. (1993). *Groups: A manual (and handouts) for chemical dependency and psychiatric treatment.* Sante Fe, NM: CL Productions.

Recovery plan outline

The recovery plan is a 90-day contract that you make with yourself, specifically detailing the action that you will take in your recovery. **This is a commitment.** To ensure success it needs to be realistic, so KEEP IT SIMPLE!

A commitment is a decision. The best way to express a commitment is to firmly state what your action will be. The words "I will" shows a decision to follow through with ACTION. For example, note the difference in the following two statements:

"I will go to a group meeting every day for 90 days."
vs.
"I will *try* to go to a group meeting every day."

In the Step programs they say, *"Trying is lying"* or, *"Trying is dying."* Trying means that there is really no commitment at all! We can always let ourselves off the hook with, *"Oh well, I tried."* Our commitment should be **simple, clean, and realistic**. For instance, if I am considering some form of exercise and I have been a "couch potato" for the last five years, then a commitment to run ten miles a day is unreasonable. Instead, I could commit to walking a few blocks every day. This could consist of a ten minute walk each way and my commitment then would be: *"I will walk a total of twenty minutes, five days per week."* Therefore, this statement includes **what I will do** and **how often I will do it**.

The following outline may help to design your own individual recovery plan:

ALWAYS INCLUDE <u>WHAT YOU WILL DO</u> AND <u>HOW OFTEN</u>!!!!

1. What will I do:

Example:

> *"I will remain chemically free, one day at a time. I will inform my physician that I am a recovering alcoholic. I will inform my dentist that I am a recovering alcoholic. I will check out all medication I may need with my sponsor or the treatment program."*

2. Meetings: When, where, and how often will you go to meetings?

Example:

"I will attend 90 meetings in 90 days." If you already know that you can't attend a meeting on a certain day, "double up" the following day. Include a tentative meeting schedule.

Example:

"I will attend 90 meetings in 90 days. Every other Monday I have class so I can't make a meeting. Therefore, I will double up meetings on Tuesday by attending the noon and 6 PM meetings."

Exercise, Continued

3. Sponsorship: Who is my sponsor? How often will I contact him/her? If I do not have a sponsor, will I get one? When will I get one?

Examples:

1. If I have a sponsor: My sponsor's name is Ann. I will call her every other day.

2. If I don't have a sponsor: I will have a sponsor in one week.

3. I am moving to Atlanta when I leave treatment. I will have a temporary sponsor within two weeks of my arrival.

4. Working The Steps:

Examples:

1. I will review my Step One with my sponsor next week.

2. I will continue working the Steps and meeting with my sponsor every two weeks.

(Remember, you cannot complete this one unless you have consulted with your sponsor.)

5. Spirituality: How do you get in touch with your spiritual self and have time for contemplation? Include a plan for prayer and meditation and/or religious practices, if appropriate.

Examples:

1. I will read _____ every morning.

2. I will pray every morning and every evening.

3. I will attend church services every two weeks with my family.

4. I will take a walk in the woods once a week.

6. Physical Health: Include commitment for diet, exercise, and medical problems.

Examples:

1. I will continue treatment for my gastric ulcer and will follow-up with my physician. I have an appointment on _____.

2. I will eat at least two healthy meals per day.

3. I will work out at the gym two times per week.

4. I will take my high blood pressure medication as prescribed by my physician.

Exercise, Continued

7. Emotional Health: Include any counseling appointments and the name of the counselor or whom you will talk with about your feelings.

Examples:

1. I will talk to my sponsor at least two times per week about my feelings.

2. I will share my feelings with my husband as they come up instead of holding them in.

3. I will follow through with my counseling appointment with _____ on _____.

Identify the feeling that is most difficult for you to deal with.

Examples: Anger

When you are angry, what will you do to deal with it?

1. Go to group and talk about it.

2. Call my sponsor, mentor, or a sober friend.

3. When I have a fight with my wife, I will go for a ten-minute walk to calm down.

4. I will practice the anger exercises in my workbook.

8. Employment: What are your work plans? Since overworking is often a compulsive behavior and can interfere with your program, what is the maximum number of hours you will work per week?

Examples:

1. If overworking is a problem: I will return to my job and will not work over 45 hours in a week.

2. If unemployment is a problem: I will begin looking for a job in one week. I will apply to at least two places per week.

3. If my job is unhealthy: I will quit my bartending job immediately.

9. Legal Issues: Include court dates and planning.

Examples:

1. I will attend my DUI hearing on _____.

2. I have an appointment with my lawyer on _____.

3. I have no legal issues pending.

Exercise, Continued

10. Family Relationships: Include a plan for activities with family members **and** a plan for dealing with using family members.

Examples:

1. I will go out to dinner or to a movie with my wife once a week.

2. I will plan an activity with my children every Saturday.

3. I will call my brother and tell him I cannot have drinking in my house when he comes to visit.

4. I will not attend my cousin's wedding next week since there will be alcohol there.

11. Social Growth: This is a plan for developing sober relationships and for detaching from using ones. What will you do to make sober friends?

Examples:

1. I will call Jake from my treatment group two times a week.

2. I will go out for coffee with my sponsor or safe friend one time a week.

3. I will go to a recovery conference in Phoenix in October.

4. I will contact Lenny to tell him that I quit my addiction and that I won't be around anymore.

12. Leisure Time: What will you do for fun? What interests or hobbies do you plan on resuming now that you are sober?

Examples:

1. I will go fishing at least once a month.

2. I will attend art classes one time per week.

3. I will hike every two weeks with a friend.

4. I will practice my guitar twice a week for one hour.

13. Fire Drill: This is your action plan for when you feel like acting out again.

Example:

1. I will call my sponsor, accountability partner.

2. I will double up my meetings for three days and talk about my craving.

Exercise, Continued

    3. I will read recovery-based literature.

    4. I will talk about it with my wife/husband.

    5. I will read my Step One.

14. Relapse Plan: If I use, what can I do **now** to keep me in recovery?

Examples:

    1. Call my sponsor or alternate if my sponsor is not available.

    2. Tell my family within 24 hours.

    3. Restart 90 meetings in 90 days, or restart a recovery group most associated with my particular addiction.

    4. Tell my Aftercare Group.

Adapted with modifications, from: Olsen, J., Fallon, J., & Mark, L. (1993). *Groups: A manual (and handouts) for chemical dependency and psychiatric treatment.* Sante Fe, NM: CL Productions.

Recovery plan worksheet

Now that you have reviewed the way a plan should look, personalize a realistic one for yourself. Make sure to designate someone to keep you accountable. Give that person a copy of your plan as well.

1. Goal or behavior to change:

2. Meeting/Group:

DAY	TIME	LOCATION
Sunday		
Monday		
Tuesday		
Wednesday		
Thursday		
Friday		
Saturday		

3. Sponsorship:

4. Working the Steps:

5. Spiritual Practice:

6. Physical Health:

7. Emotional Health:

The emotion that places me at greatest risk for reactive behavior is:

THE STAGES OF CHANGE WORKBOOK

Exercise, Continued

When I feel _____, I will:

    a.

    b.

    c.

8. **Employment:**

9. **Legal Issues:**

10. **Family Relationships:**

11. **Social Growth:**

12. **Leisure Activities:**

13. **Fire Drill: Five things I will do if I feel vulnerable to a set back:**

a.

b.

c.

d.

e.

Exercise, Continued

14. Relapse Plan: Things that I will do if I relapse:

a.

b.

c.

d.

e.

Adapted with modifications, from: Olsen, J., Fallon, J., & Mark, L. (1993). *Groups: A manual (and handouts) for chemical dependency and psychiatric treatment.* Sante Fe, NM: CL Production.

A Deeper Look

The Action stage requires that we live meaningful and fulfilling lives. One way to do that is to be mindful of how we look at things. Mindfulness is noticing what we don't normally notice because our heads are too busy with worry, the past, what we need to do, or dreading mistakes.

The act of mindfulness training helps us to take another look; being mindful of the here and now, and to regroup toward greater harmony. Mindfulness brings on new pleasures.

Practice:

Be aware of your body, your emotions, and what is happening at the moment. Notice sensations, identify cues that will bring you back to mindfulness – such as a church bell. Reduce any distractions and busyness and practice living in the moment in peace and harmony, not worry or dread.

Follow up:

To improve your practice, read material on Mindfulness, and learn more. Conduct a search engine search (e.g. Google) for: "Mindfulness Training". There are several good free sites that offer helpful information. For example, UCLA offers free online classes on Mindfulness Training (See: http://marc.ucla.edu/body.cfm?id=76)

See also this workbook, available for purchase:

Teasdale, T. (2014). *The mindful way workbook*. New York: Guildford Press.

Setting Goals: Using the SMART Model

A good format for goal setting is the SMART format. SMART stands for: specific, measurable, attainable, realistic, and time-bound. Blank sheets that you can fill out are available on the public domain at:

http://www.uwlax.edu/hr/current/idp/Smart%20Goal%20Worksheet.pdf

or

https://www.hnfs.com/content/dam/hnfs/tn/bene/wellness/flash/HW1111x103_readiness.swf

For this exercise complete a SMART plan for your established goal.

Example:

Specific: *I want to be able to attend a support group to help me deal with co-dependency.*
Measurable: *Yes, each meeting last 60 minutes x 3 a week.*
Attainable: *Yes, I am ready and meetings are available.*
Realistic: *Yes, there are 3 meetings a week in the evening and I am free then.*
Time-bound: *I will attend 1 meeting a week starting next Monday.*

Chapter 6   Exercises for maintenance

Practical tasks:

- Plan for follow-up support

- Reinforcement of internal rewards

- Discuss relapse prevention

Practicing H.AL.T

H.A.L.T. is an acronym that stands for Hungry, Angry, Lonely, and Tired. It is often used in recovery circles. The items stand for the red flags to acting out. In other words, when you are lonely, you are most vulnerable to a fall. To prevent this, you need an action plan. The action plan can be both proactive/preventive and reactive/curative. The proactive/preventive plan helps you avoid getting lonely. A reactive/curative plan is when it's too late and loneliness has already peaked its evil head. You will then need to know what to do. In this exercise you are asked to set up both a proactive/preventive and a reactive/curative plan using the H.A.L.T. acronym.

I: Proactive/preventive plan. What I will do to avoid the following from taking its toll:

Hungry – _____

Angry – _____

Lonely – _____

Tired – _____

II: Reactive/curative plan. What I will do when the following takes its toll:

Hungry – _____

Angry – _____

Lonely – _____

Tired – _____

Relapse warning signs

There are no automatic guarantees in recovery. You live one day at a time. However, there are some warning signs to relapse, and if you stay conscious of them, you improve your opportunity not to relapse.

I. Use the following inventory to identify common relapse warning signs.

_____ Trying to control/ run another's recovery program

_____ Isolation

_____ Depression

_____ Compulsive or impulsive behaviors

_____ Attempts to control people, places, and things

_____ Being defensive

_____ "I don't care" attitude

_____ Taking on the responsibilities of others

_____ Easily angered

_____ Daydreaming

_____ Lying

_____ Holding feelings in

_____ Periods of confusion

_____ Feeling powerless and hopeless

_____ Feeling sorry for myself

_____ Preoccupation with one area of my life

_____ Over-reaction to stressful situations

_____ Over or under sleeping

_____ Over or under eating

_____ Loss of daily structure

_____ Feelings of inferiority or superiority

_____ Nagging/whining

_____ Immature wish to be happy or to make others happy

_____ Insensitivity to the feelings of others

Exercise, Continued

_____ Avoiding issues or problems

_____ Try to force sobriety on others

_____ Focusing on the past

_____ Projecting into the future

_____ Not having any fun

_____ Compulsive sexual behavior

_____ Hoarding money or overspending

_____ Increasing physical complaints

_____ Fantasies about the addiction behaviors

_____ Increasing work dissatisfaction

_____ Overconfidence about recovery

_____ Increasing use of non-prescription medication

_____ Rejecting help

_____ Blaming others for my problems

_____ Cutting down or stopping meetings

_____ Resentments

_____ Hanging around addiction stimuli/environments

_____ Thinking I am *cured*

_____ Start using a chemical other than my drug of choice

_____ Convince myself I can practice "controlled" behaviors

_____ Losing control

_____ Deny my fears

_____ See problems as unsolvable

_____ Unrealistic expectations

II. Review those you checked and complete a Relapse Prevention Plan (see page 56).

THE STAGES OF CHANGE WORKBOOK

Stress management

Candi Raudebaugh, owner and operator of *Inner Health Studio*, is a producer of relaxation podcasts and downloads. Raudebaugh (2013) has provided a comprehensive list of coping strategies for effective stress management. In this exercise review and apply Raudebaugh's list of effective stress management methods:

> **Decrease stress at its source**. *If relationships are causing stress, working on setting boundaries or on becoming more assertive may be helpful. If too many demands on your time are causes of stress for you, it may be beneficial to work on setting priorities and limits, and cut back on things that you're able to let go for the time being.*

> **Physical activity**. *Physical activity helps to use up the excess energy produced by the stress response. In fight-or-flight mode, the body is ready for intense physical activity. By exercising, the stress response runs its course, and the body returns to a physiological normal.*

> **Creativity**. *Hobbies and creative outlets can be excellent stress relievers. Try out the creative expression relaxation download to experience creativity as an example of one of the many possible creative stress management exercises you can use.*

> **Take care of yourself**. *Treating yourself well is a good way to cope with stress. If you have good physical and emotional reserves, you are better prepared to handle stress that comes your way. Do things you enjoy, treat yourself, and talk kindly to yourself.... in other words, treat yourself like a friend.*

> **Time management**. *Managing your time effectively can significantly decrease stress. Avoid the trap of over-scheduling by prioritizing tasks and putting free time into your schedule.*

> **Decrease procrastination**. *Procrastination can add to your stress - when things are put off, you are always working under pressure, which is stressful! Using a schedule and rewarding yourself are ways to prevent procrastination.*

> **Sleep**. *Make sure you are getting enough sleep. Even a few hours of missed sleep affects your memory and concentration significantly.*

> **Reward yourself**. *Plan to treat yourself after completing a task. Rewards do not have to be extravagant. A reward can be a simple, small treat like watching a movie, taking a warm bath, playing a game, or listening to music.*

> **Relaxation**. *Relaxation is a very effective way to calm your mind and relax your body. Relaxation techniques such as progressive muscle relaxation, visualization, and guided meditation are some of the best stress management exercises you can use. When you feel more relaxed you will be able to be more productive. Listening to guided relaxation often helpful for learning to relax.*

> *Visit* **http://www.innerhealthstudio.com** *for free relaxation downloads to try guided relaxation.*

Centering

In this exercise you will connect with your body and mind. You will become present and relaxed in the situation.

1. Sit in a chair with your back straight, or lie flat on the floor with your palms facing the ceiling. You can do this in silence or with affirmation tapes or music.

2. Focus your attention on the center of your chest, or some other safe focal point.

3. Breath in and out easily and completely. The inhalation should be shorter than the exhalation.

4. On the exhalation, think of pushing the air out completely and in the inhalation, allow the breath to re-enter the body.

5. Imagine the inhalation as being ease and light and the exhalation as a release of toxic energy.

Do this until you feel centered and relaxed.

What does a healthy support system look like?

Members in a healthy support system should have certain characteristics. Be sure when choosing members of your support network, that they have these minimal characteristics.

- Members are not substance abusers.
- Members are trustworthy.
- Members are mature.
- Members should know you fairly well.
- Members should be able to confront you.
- Members should be able to keep you accountable.
- Members should be available to you when you need, and when busy, be responsible to get back to you in a reasonable time period.
- Members communicate well.
- Member are willing to listen in a supportive way.

II: After ensuring the above, complete the exercise "Identifying my support network" on page 77.

Journaling

During recovery you will need to release thoughts and feelings in a constructive, safe way. Journaling is one way to help bring unconscious material conscious. It helps keep you present. It is a tool to gain insight into oneself.

1. Use the journaling sheets provided at the end of this workbook to journal your thoughts and feelings. You may also find it helpful to purchase a separate notebook to do this exercise.

2. Allow whatever you are feeling to surface without thinking about it-just let it come.

3. Put your feelings into words and write them down without trying to sound proper or nice; editing and grammar is not necessary. Do not distract the real emotions from coming.

Identifying my support network

Now that you are maintaining some lasting change, ask yourself who helped you get where you are today.

In this exercise identify those people who have helped you get where you are now. It is these people you will need to continuity of contact, and to call on when you feel you might spiral downward.

My Support List:

<u>Name</u>   <u>Contact info</u>

Asking for forgiveness

Asking for forgiveness is part of a healthy recovery process. In step eight of the Twelve Step Traditions, it states that someone in recovery should be willing to make amends when possible.

Here are the four steps in asking for forgiveness.

1. *Acknowledge the injury.* It's important to start by acknowledging that you have injured someone. A simple, "I know that I hurt your feelings," can make a world of difference.

2. *Ask the injured what it was like for them.* It's important to understand in what way your mistake injured the other person. People are very different. The same mistake can injure people in a wide variety of ways. Taking the time to understand the manner in which you injured someone else increases empathy in your relationship. Ask what hurt. Nothing is more frustrating than being told how someone who gets it wrong hurt you! Repeat back what you heard to make sure you did not miss anything. Open your heart to hear the actual injury.

3. *Apologize for the injury.* Be specific. Make sure to include all the ways that you injured the other person. A real apology might sound like, "I am sorry that I hurt your feelings and you felt stupid when I ignored you at dinner." A real apology includes, "I am sorry" for a "specific injury" at a "specific time".

4. *Ask the injured how you can make it better.* When we feel guilty, we often desperately want to repair the relationship. In our anxiety and fear of losing the relationship, we make up ways to repair the relationship. Stop working so hard. Ask the injured what you can do to regain their trust. Most people have a clear idea of what you can do; ask them. Follow these easy steps and watch your relationships improve. Apologies are the backbone of relationships. This simple skill will greatly impact all of your relationships. Start today. You are bound to make some mistake today. Practice your new skill. You'll be surprised at the results.

Reference: Editor, The lost art of apology. *The Open Grove*, 5(9B), 1.

Good-bye letter to your addiction, or problem

Whether you like to think of it this way of not, you have had a relationship with your addiction or problem(s). It has been an arena full of excitements and letdowns; the *status quo*. It has occupied a lot of your time, whether it was in your head or in acting-out activities. At some point you have to put an end to your relationship with it. It is much like a divorce. While it is best to leave it, there will be some pain involved. It is a voluntary decision. If you are ready to say goodbye to it, then write a good-bye letter. Tell it what it did to you, what you won't miss, and the new joy you'll have. Share your grief, what you'll miss about it, what adaptations it served for you. Tell it how it has been replaced. Finally, tell it how it needs to go way and how you will live your life without it.

Dear _____

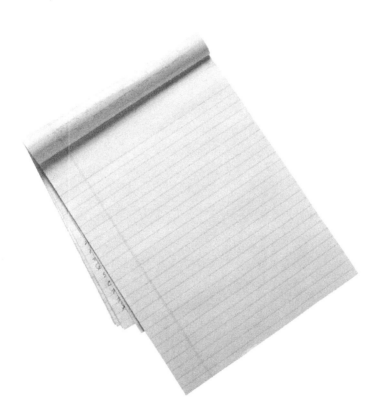

Become a champion for change

After you have faced growth and change, you will want to give back. In this exercise you will think about ways to give back to others that which you have gained for yourself.

Some ideas include:

- Rejoice and celebrate soberly!

- Start a support group, or other worthy cause.

- Become a mentor.

- Give to groups that assist and advocate change.

- Share your story with an individual or any size audience.

- Volunteer at a recovery seminar or retreat. Give back!

- Write and share your story.

- Partner with others to build a stronger community.

- Encourage and inspire others.

Continued growth and development

What keeps you growing and developing? This is a vital question to ask yourself and may need refining. In this exercise list those learning events and activities that are needed to help you to continue to grow and develop. This is not a one-time exercise, it should be updated periodically.

I: Learning (what classes, books, websites, apps, etc. can I turn to help me continue in my growth and development?):

II: Activities (what activities can I do to help me further grow and develop?):

Chapter 7 Exercises for relapse/prevention

Practical Tasks:

-Evaluate triggers for relapse

-Reassess motivation and barriers

-Plan stronger coping strategies

-Reassess and rewrite relapse prevention plan

Is this what I really want?

Relapse is a reality. It can be an opportunity to assess how you feel about change; about what led to the relapse to old behaviors, and enable you to consider again whether you have had enough and if you really want change. In this exercise you will be given the opportunity to assess how you feel as it relates to the relapse and provide a framework to work through your readiness for change now.

Summarize your feelings and thought as it relates to your relapse:

Do you feel you want to continue the behaviors, or return to changing them?

List any positive attributes to the relapse:

List any negative attributes, or consequences that may have resulted:

Summarize what you learned:

Preventing future relapse

Relapse is common. It's best to regroup and not loss hope when a relapse occurs. To help prevent future relapse, its best to rethink and rewrite your Recovery plan worksheet. Take time to do that now (See page 64).

Building coping skills against relapse

Miller and Harris (2002) found that a lack of coping skills is predictive of relapse. So, how do you build coping skills? Professional counselor Lori Clancy (2013) author of the website "Help for hurting people," discusses the *wagon wheel* approach. Clancy asserts that a wagon wheel has to have many solid spokes for it to roll without fail. In this exercise review and apply Clancy's ideal list for how to add spokes to your own wagon wheel:

1. **Look for hidden resources in your neighborhood**. There may be an older person in the neighborhood that you could visit with and learn from. You may also have a group, AA, or self-help group in your neighborhood.

2. **Common Interests**. If you used to hike, look for a hiking club. If you like sports, find a local league- or watching them – visit with those around you. If you like books, join a new book club. If you don't have any interests right now – you are in an exciting place… experiment until you find something you like.

3. **Be creative**. If you keep looking for supports in the same place and haven't been finding them, look somewhere else.

4. **Volunteer**. Schools, churches, non-profit agencies are always looking for help and it is a great way to build relationships. If you love animals, go to an animal shelter and walk the animals, start building relationships.

5. **Hang out in new places**. Coffee shops, book stores, places that invite you to hang out and are healthy for you to hang out are great places to meet new people and find some common interests. Sometimes just going to a place that has good memories is a support.

6. **Build your faith**. People who have a faith have a built in support system – many times through the church or meetings that they attend. Church can be a great place to meet new people and have support.

7. **Professional resources**. There are always professional mentors, counselors, treatment groups that can be a huge resource for many people that need direction.

8. **Families**. So many times families are disconnected you may have a relative that could be a great resource for you that you have not contacted in a while. Remember to screen family members – make sure they are a healthy resource.

Identifying high risk situations

Frequent exposure to what is referred to as "high risk" situations can make you more susceptible to relapsing to former behavior. High-risk situations are individualistic, what is high risk for one person may not be for another. Whatever it is for you, its best to avoid them, but if they cannot be avoided, then you must learn to cope with them.

The first step is to recognize when you are in, or close to a risky situation. It is important to learn to pay attention to the situations you find yourself in and practice being aware of changes in your thoughts and feelings.

Practical:

Take time now and identify three high-risk situations. It may help to think back to your last relapse and picture the situation just before you decided to act out.

Identifying problem areas

Relapse recovery requires identifying and taking care of life's problem areas. These can be specific to work, home, or relational. This exercise gives you an opportunity to inventory key areas of you life and to think about what is problematic.

Work/school (e.g. grades slipping; pressures with boss):

_____
_____
_____
_____
_____

Home (e.g. home repairs; bills increasing):

_____
_____
_____
_____
_____

Relational (e.g. spouse cheating; communication):

_____
_____
_____
_____
_____

What did my relapse teach me?

While relapse can be frustrating and disappointing, it can be an opportunity to learn more about yourself and how to prevent future problems. If you have relapsed, take the time to write a narrative about your experience. Key in on the things you learned, your feelings involved and thoughts about how you might do things differently now with this knowledge. Use the journal pages in the back of this book, or use a personal diary or notebook if you wish.

Rebounding from relapse

Relapse is difficult for sure, and it can also play serious head games with you. After relapse, some people just want to throw in the towel saying, "What's the use, I failed again!" But, think of it as an opportunity to rebound, to move forward, not backwards. In this exercise review and practice some of these things you can do to rebound from a relapse:

1. Alert you support system – ask them to increase accountability and support. Relationships really matter in a time like this. The worst thing you can do is isolate.

2. Write about your experience noting what you learned.

3. Make plans to celebrate your halt! Yes, you relapsed, but celebrate that you have stopped that behavior, too! Treat yourself to a prize such as a night out to the movies, the spa, a nice meal, or a treat.

4. Reconnect with any activities or support networks you may have neglected.

5. Reach out and help others. Once you are back on track, it helps to give back.

6. Evaluate the necessary adjustment s you need to make to stay on track.

7. Remind yourself why you changed in the first place. Keep this in the forefront. Remind yourself why change is so important to you and your loved ones. Refresh yourself with these thoughts verses the dread of the relapse itself.

8. Update your relapse prevention plan if you need to. Ask yourself why it failed. Make the necessary adjustments.

9. Clean out the house again. Get rid of any physical triggers that may still linger.

10. Relax! Yes, take it easy and most of all don't beat yourself up. This will only set you up for future problems.

RELAPSE prevention

Use the acronym **RELAPSE** to help you avoid relapse:

Renew: Take time to take care of yourself. This may mean getting rest, or taking a break.

Exercise: Use the exercises in this workbook, or others similar

Limit: Limit exposure to former triggers

Appreciate: Use self-affirmations (see page 8)

Plan: Use the relapse prevention plans you complete in this workbook (see page 56)

Strategize: Ask what you can do when you are feeling stuck.

Reset the clock

If you relapse you do not have to start all over. Remember you gain a lot along the way before relapse. After relapse most people feel like they have failed and have to start all over again. Think of relapse as a restart of the clock, not a total do over. In this exercise you will reassess and think about all the work and progress you had before relapse. This assessment will renew your purpose.

Strides I made before I relapsed:

Things I accomplished before my relapse:

What I learned before my relapse:

Warning signs

Experience shows that there are correlates to relapse. Some of these are common and listed below.

I: Review some of the coming warning signs to relapse. Then list what might be your own:

- Stopping medication on one's own, or against the advice of medical professionals.
- Hanging around in old places and with old friends.
- Isolating – not attending meetings/not using the telephone for support.
- Keeping vices around the house.
- Obsessive thinking about addictive substances.
- Failing to follow one's treatment plan – stopping therapy or skipping the doctors.
- Feeling over confident – that you no longer need support.
- Relationship problems – ongoing serious conflicts with someone who still does unhealthy behaviors.
- Setting unrealistic goals – being too hard on yourself.
- Changes in eating and sleeping patterns, personal hygiene, or energy levels.
- Feeling overwhelmed confused and stressed out.
- Constant boredom, irritability and lack or routine and structure in life.
- Sudden changes in psychiatric symptoms.
- Dwelling on resentments and past hurts – anger – unresolved conflicts.
- Avoidance – refusing to deal with personal issues, and other problems of daily living.
- Engaging in obsessive behaviors – workaholic/gambling/sexual excess/over eating excess.
- Major life changes: loss/grief/trauma/painful emotions.
- Ignoring relapse warning signs and triggers.

II: List your own person warning signs:

Dress rehearsal

A concentration on possible high-risk situations and effective strategies to deal with them will enhance self-efficiency and help prevent further relapse. In this exercise list those possible high-risk situations you are familiar with and then list those strategies you can use to counteract them.

High-risk situations	Counter-acting strategies

References and suggested readings

Alcoholics Anonymous. (1975). *Living Sober.* New York: Author.

Alcoholics Anonymous (2007). The Big Book (online version): http://www.alcoholics-anonymous.org/bigbookonline/

Bradshaw, J. (1987). *Healing the shame that binds you.* Deerfield Beach, FL: Health Communications.

Bradshaw, J. (1992). *Homecoming: Reclaiming and championing your inner child.* New York: Bantam Doubleday Dell.

Burns, D (1989). *The feeling good handbook.* New York: Quill/HarperCollins

Burns, D. (1993). Ten *days to self esteem.* New York: Quill/HarperCollins.

Backus, W. (1987). *Finding the freedom of self-control.* Minneapolis: Bethany House.

Capacchione, L. (1991). *Recovery of your inner child.* New York: Fireside Books.

Campbell, S. (2001). *Getting real.* Tiburon, CA: HJ Kramer

Carnes, P. (1992). *Out of the shadows: Understanding sexual addiction.* Center City, MN: Hazelden.

Clancy, L. (2013). *Positive coping skills: Wagon wheel supports.* Retrieved from http://helpforthehurting.net/wagon-wheel-supports/

Fanning, P. & O'Neill, J. T. (2004). *The addiction workbook: A step-by-step guide to quitting alcohol and drugs.* Oakland, CA: New Harbinger.

Felgen, J. (2007). *Leading lasting change.* Minneapolis, MN: Creative Health Care Management.

Fossum, M. A. & Mason, M. J. (1986). *Facing shame: Families in recovery.* New York: W. W. Norton.

Gorski, T. T. (1989). *Passages through time: An action plan for preventing relapse.* New York: Harper/Hazelden.

Gorski, T. T., & Trundy, A. B. (2000). *Relapse prevention workbook: Practical exercises for managing high-risk situations.* Independence, MO: Herald Publishing.

Greenberger, D. & Padesky, C. A. (1995). *Mind over mood.* New York: Guilford Press.

Horvath, T. (2004). *Sex, drugs, gambling, and chocolate.* Atascadero, CA: Impact Publishers.

Katherine, A. (1991). *Anatomy of a food addiction: An effective program to overcome compulsive eating.* Carlsbad, CA: Gurze Books.

Lerner, R. (1990). *Affirmation for the inner child.* Deerfield, FL: Health Communications, Inc.

Marlatt, G.A., & Daley, D. C. (1997). *Managing your drug or alcohol problem: Client workbook.* San Antonio: Psychological Corporation.

Miller, A. (1996). *The drama of the gifted child: The search for the true self.* New York: Basic Books.

Miller, W. R., & Harris, R. J. (2002). What predicts relapse? Prospective testing of antecedent models. *Addiction.* Retrieved from http://onlinelibrary.wiley.com/doi/10.1046/j.1360-0443.91.12s1.7.x/abstract

Miller, W. R., & Rollnick, S. (2013). *Motivational interviewing: Helping people change* (3rd edition). New York, NY: Guilford.

Minirth, F. B. (1981). *The workaholic and his family.* Grand Rapids, MI: Baker.

Narcotics Anonymous (1982). *The blue book.* Chatsworth CA: Narcotics Anonymous.

Noll, S. (1992). *Songs for the inner child* [CD]. Santa Fe, NM: Singing Heart Productions.

Perkinson, R. R. (2003). *The gambling addiction patient workbook.* Thousand Oaks, CA: Sage.

Phelan, J. E. (2011). The addictions recovery workbook: 101 practical exercises for individuals and groups. Charleston, SC: Practical Application Publications. https://www.createspace.com/3581171

Potter-Efron, R. & Potter-Efron, P. (1989). *Letting go of shame: Understanding how shame affects your life.* Center City, MN: Hazelden.

Prochaska J. O., & DiClemente, C. C. (1984). *The Transtheoretical approach: Towards a systematic eclectic framework.* Homewood, IL: Dow Jones Irwin.

Raudebaugh, C. (2013). *Healthy coping with stress.* Retrieved from http://www.innerhealthstudio.com/stress-management-exercises.html

Ridgeway, P., McDiarmid, D., Davidson, L., Bayes, J., & Ratzlaft, S. (2006). *Pathways to recovery: A strengths recovery self-help workbook.* Lawrence, KS: University of Kansas, School of Social Welfare.

Rogers, R. L. & McMillin, C. S. (1992). *Relapse traps: How to avoid the 12 most common pitfalls in recovery.* New York: Bantam.

Schaeffer, B. (1997). *Is it love, or is it addiction?* Center City, MN: Hazelden.

Schaeffer, B. (1998). *Inner reflections: Meditations for the body and heart* [CD]. Center City, MN: Hazelden.

Teasdale, T. (2014). *The mindful way workbook.* New York: Guildford Press.

Twerski, A. (1990). *Addictive thinking: Understanding self-deception.* New York: Harper/Hazelden.

Weiser, J. (1993). *Phototherapy techniques: Exploring the secrets of personal snapshots and family albums.* San Francisco: Jossey-Bass.

Important Contacts Quick Reference

Name	Address	Phone	Web

(Sponsor)

Journal

Journal

Journal

Journal

Journal

Journal

Journal

Journal

Journal

Journal

Journal

Journal

Journal

Journal

Journal

Other Books by this author:

*"The Addictions Workbook:
101 Practical Exercises for Individuals and Groups"*

Order from:

https://www.createspace.com/3581171

Made in United States
North Haven, CT
18 April 2025

68068129R00070